Asteroid

CHERRY LAKE PRESS

Published in the United States of America by Cherry Lake Publishing
Ann Arbor, Michigan
www.cherrylakepublishing.com

Reading Adviser: Beth Walker Gambro, MS, Ed., Reading Consultant, Yorkville, IL
Book Design: Jennifer Wahi
Illustrator: Jeff Bane

Photo Credits: © adventtr/iStock.com, 5; © Vadim Sadovski/Shutterstock.com, 7; © Nazarii_Neshcherenskyi/Shutterstock.com, 9; © Dotted Yeti/Shutterstock.com, 11; © 24K-Production/Shutterstock.com, 13; © PIA11735/NASA, 15; © Jurik Peter/Shutterstock.com, 17; © Mode-list/iStock.com, 19; © Sergey Nivens/Shutterstock.com, 21; © Artsiom P/Shutterstock.com, 23; Cover, 2-3, 8, 18, 22, 24, Jeff Bane

Cherry Lake Press is an imprint of Cherry Lake Publishing Group.

Library of Congress Cataloging-in-Publication Data

Names: Devera, Czeena, author. | Bane, Jeff, 1957- illustrator.
Title: Asteroid / by Czeena Devera ; illustrated by Jeff Bane.
Description: Ann Arbor, Michigan : Cherry Lake Publishing, [2022] | Series: My guide to the solar system | Audience: Grades K-1 |
Identifiers: LCCN 2021036515 (print) | LCCN 2021036516 (ebook) | ISBN 9781534198999 (hardcover) | ISBN 9781668900130 (paperback) | ISBN 9781668901571 (pdf) | ISBN 9781668905890 (ebook)
Subjects: LCSH: Asteroids--Juvenile literature.
Classification: LCC QB651 .D48 2022 (print) | LCC QB651 (ebook) | DDC 523.44--dc23
LC record available at https://lccn.loc.gov/2021036515
LC ebook record available at https://lccn.loc.gov/2021036516

Printed in the United States of America
Corporate Graphics

About the author: Czeena Devera grew up in the red-hot heat of Arizona surrounded by books. Her childhood bedroom had built-in bookshelves that were always full. She now lives in Michigan with an even bigger library of books.

About the illustrator: Jeff Bane and his two business partners own a studio along the American River in Folsom, California, home of the 1849 Gold Rush. When Jeff's not sketching or illustrating for clients, he's either swimming or kayaking in the river to relax.

I'm an **asteroid**. I live in outer space.

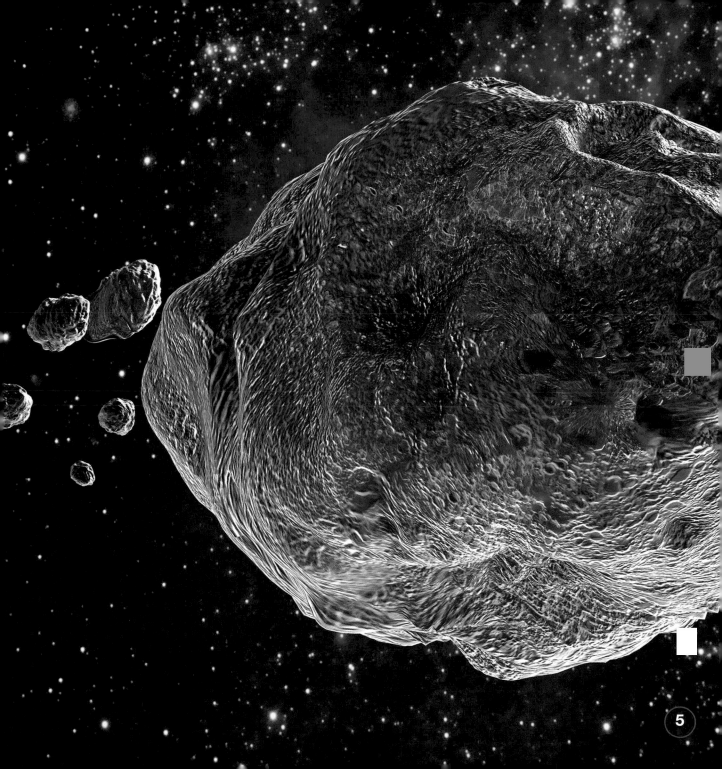

I'm about 4.6 billion years old.
I formed at the same time as the
solar system.

How would you describe yourself?

I'm lumpy. I have **craters**. Some people say I look like a potato.

There are many others like me. We come in different sizes. We can be as tall as a refrigerator. Or we can be as tall as the Egyptian pyramids.

Some asteroids are really, really large. They're called **minor** planets.

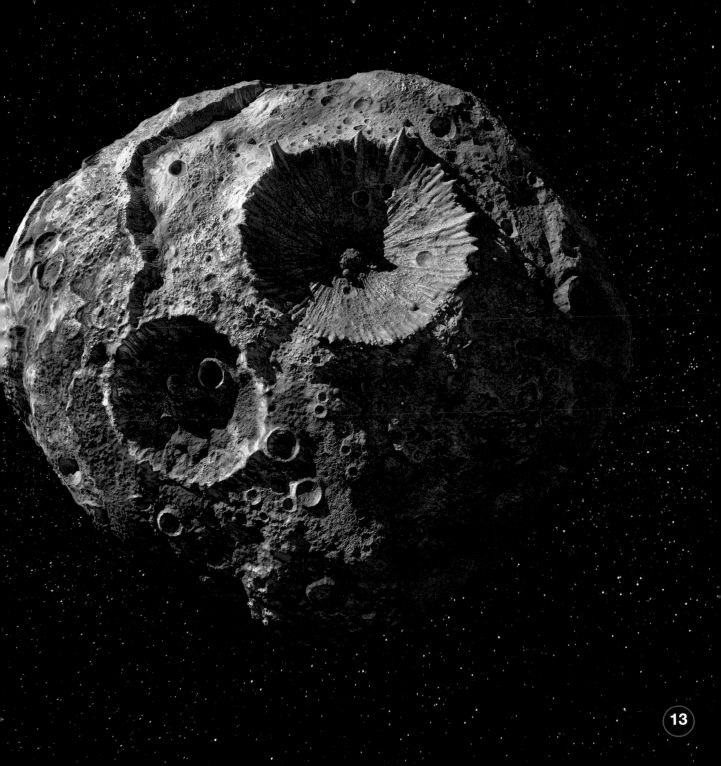

Sometimes we crash and bump into each other. This can make us break into smaller sizes.

We come in three types. These are **carbon**, stony, and metallic asteroids.

We **orbit** the Sun. Our orbit follows the same direction as the planets.

Most of us orbit the Sun in a ring. This is called the asteroid belt. It's between Mars and Jupiter.

Scientists are still studying me. There's so much more to learn!

glossary

asteroid (AH-stuh-royd) one of thousands of rocky objects that move in orbits mostly between the planets Mars and Jupiter

carbon (KAR-buhn) a chemical element

craters (KRAY-tuhrs) holes formed by an impact

minor (MYE-nuhr) small or not important

orbit (OR-buht) to travel in a curved path around something, such as a planet or star

scientists (SYE-uhn-tists) people who study nature and the world we live in

solar system (SOH-luhr SIH-stuhm) a star and the planets that move around it

index